ARE YOU MY LOVER?
WORKBOOK

A COMPANION GUIDE FOR SHADOW WORK, MIRROR WORK, AND SELF LOVE

BY DR. KEZIA SHINE

SETTING THE STAGE

Before we can truly begin, it is important to remember that this workbook is not just a set of exercises, it is a mirror. Every question, every reflection, every ritual is an invitation to look deeper into yourself. The stories in *Are You My Lover?* may feel whimsical or even lighthearted at first, but beneath them lives a powerful truth: the relationships we choose, and the partners we are drawn to, reveal the parts of ourselves still waiting to be healed.

So often, we look outward for love. We chase the promise of fulfillment through someone else's embrace, believing that if we just find "the one," everything will finally make sense. Yet time and again, many of us discover that the very people we choose bring us face-to-face with pain, abandonment, confusion, or disappointment. And while it is easy to blame them-or to blame ourselves-the deeper truth is that these experiences are not punishments. They are lessons. Each relationship is a teacher, a mirror reflecting back to us the shadows we carry and the wounds we have not yet tended.

Doing this inner work matters because until we see those shadows clearly, they continue to shape our choices. Without awareness, we repeat cycles: chasing after thrill-seekers, falling for charmers, clinging to protectors, or losing ourselves in the chaos of storms. These patterns are not coincidences-they are invitations. Life keeps placing the same lessons in our path until we are ready to see, ready to learn, and ready to choose differently.

Healing begins when we stop asking, "Why did they treat me this way?" and begin asking, "What is this showing me about myself?" It begins when we turn inward with compassion instead of judgment, when we stop running from the pain and instead sit with it, listen to it, and love the parts of us that ache. That is the essence of shadow work: to face the hidden parts of ourselves with courage, and to allow the light of awareness to transform them.

This workbook is designed to support you in that process. Each archetype you will meet here is more than a character from a story. They are reflections of energies, patterns, and wounds you may have encountered in your own relationships. Through journaling, mirror work, and release rituals, you will uncover what these patterns have been trying to teach you. And by the time you arrive at the final section, you will not just understand these lessonsyou will hold yourself with more love than ever before.

Why is this important? Because true love cannot be found until it is lived within. Until you can look in the mirror and see yourself, really see yourself, with compassion, tenderness, and reverence, you will always be searching outside of you. The journey of this workbook is not about finding "the one" out there. It is about becoming the one for yourself.

So take a breath. Settle in. Open your heart. You are about to walk through shadow into light, through heartbreak into wholeness. This is your healing. This is your journey home to you.

INTENTION SETTING

Write down why you picked up this workbook.
What do you hope to heal?
How do you want to show up in relationships?

_____

_____

_____

_____

_____

_____

_____

_____

_____

_____

_____

_____

_____

_____

_____

_____

_____

_____

_____

_____

ARCHETYPE REFLECTIONS

Before we can love from truth, we must first meet the mirrors that have shaped us. Every partner, every connection, every heartbreak carries a reflection of something within, a belief, a fear, a longing, a forgotten part of ourselves. The Archetype Reflections are an invitation to explore those mirrors with curiosity and compassion.

These archetypes - the Adventurer, the Poet, the Protector, the Party Lover, the Storm, and the Narcissist; are not meant to define anyone as "good" or "bad."
They are energies, patterns, and teachers that reveal the dynamics we've experienced in love and the ways we've learned to seek, chase, or protect our hearts.

As you move through each archetype, notice what feelings arise. Do you recognize this energy in others you've loved, or perhaps within yourself? Let this be a process of discovery, not judgment. Each reflection offers an opportunity to understand your own story more deeply and reclaim the pieces of you that have been scattered along the way.

Take your time. Write freely. Allow your heart to speak. Some reflections may bring softness, others discomfort, but every emotion is a doorway to your healing.

Remember, the purpose of these pages is not to assign blame but to illuminate truth.
Through awareness, you bring light to your shadows.
Through compassion, you transform your pain into wisdom.
And through understanding, you begin to see that every relationship, even the ones that hurt, has been guiding you home to yourself.

THE ADVENTURER

The Adventurer is magnetic, full of life, and always chasing the next thrill. They might whisk you away on spontaneous trips, inspire you to try things you never thought you would, or challenge you to push past your comfort zones. But their constant drive for 'what's next' can leave you feeling left behind or never enough.

POTENTIAL EXPERIENCES

- Feeling swept off your feet at the beginning but struggling to keep up.

- A relationship where every moment is exciting, but nothing feels grounded.

- Feeling invisible when the next adventure calls to them.

- Realizing that in chasing their approval, you lost pieces of yourself.

When have I attracted an Adventurer?

_____

_____

_____

_____

_____

_____

_____

_____

_____

What part of me was seeking something through them?

_____

_____

_____

_____

_____

_____

_____

_____

_____

_____

_____

_____

_____

_____

_____

_____

_____

_____

_____

_____

_____

_____

What did this relationship mirror back to me?

_____

_____

_____

_____

_____

_____

_____

_____

_____

_____

_____

_____

_____

_____

_____

_____

_____

_____

_____

_____

_____

What did I gain in this connection?

_____

_____

_____

_____

_____

_____

_____

_____

_____

_____

_____

_____

_____

_____

_____

_____

_____

_____

_____

_____

_____

What did I lose in this connection?

_____

_____

_____

_____

_____

_____

_____

_____

_____

_____

_____

_____

_____

_____

_____

_____

_____

_____

_____

_____

_____

_____

MIRROR WORK

Stand in front of a mirror and say:

"I don't have to chase love.
I am worthy of love that feels steady and secure.."

Take a moment to notice what emotions or resistance rise up.
Write them here:

_____

_____

_____

_____

_____

_____

_____

_____

_____

_____

_____

_____

_____

_____

_____

RELEASE RITUAL

Write a letter to the Adventurer archetype. Thank them for the lessons, acknowledge what you are releasing, and affirm your worthiness of love that feels aligned and whole.

_____

_____

_____

_____

_____

_____

_____

_____

_____

_____

_____

_____

_____

_____

_____

_____

_____

_____

"Every person you meet is a mirror,
showing you the parts of yourself waiting to be loved"

THE POET

The Poet is dreamy, romantic, and enchanting with words. They may write you poems, sing you songs, or sweep you into their imagination. But sometimes their love exists more in fantasy than in reality, leaving you feeling unseen in the day-to-day.

POTENTIAL EXPERIENCES

- Feeling adored in words but neglected in presence.

- Swept into the beauty of their creativity,
  yet feeling lonely beside them.

- Believing in their potential while, in reality,
  never matched the dream.

- Wondering if you were loved or just part of their art.

When have I attracted a Poet?

_____

_____

_____

_____

_____

_____

_____

_____

_____

_____

_____

What part of me was seeking something through them?

_____

_____

_____

_____

_____

_____

_____

_____

_____

_____

_____

_____

_____

_____

_____

_____

_____

_____

_____

_____

_____

_____

What did this relationship mirror back to me?

_____

_____

_____

_____

_____

_____

_____

_____

_____

_____

_____

_____

_____

_____

_____

_____

_____

_____

_____

_____

What did I gain in this connection?

_____

_____

_____

_____

_____

_____

_____

_____

_____

_____

_____

_____

_____

_____

_____

_____

_____

_____

_____

What did I lose in this connection?

_____

_____

_____

_____

_____

_____

_____

_____

_____

_____

_____

_____

_____

_____

_____

_____

_____

_____

_____

_____

_____

_____

MIRROR WORK

Stand in front of a mirror and say:

*"I deserve love that stays steady in the daylight,
not just in the shadows of dreams."*

Take a moment to notice what emotions or resistance rise up.
Write them here:

_____

_____

_____

_____

_____

_____

_____

_____

_____

_____

_____

_____

_____

_____

_____

_____

RELEASE RITUAL

Write a letter to the Poet archetype. Thank them for the lessons, acknowledge what you are releasing, and affirm your worthiness of love that feels aligned and whole.

_____

_____

_____

_____

_____

_____

_____

_____

_____

_____

_____

_____

_____

_____

_____

_____

_____

_____

"Every person you meet is a mirror,
showing you the parts of yourself waiting to be loved"

THE PROTECTOR

The Protector offers safety, strength, and security. At first, it feels grounding and safe. But protection can slowly become control, building walls around you rather than bridges with you.

POTENTIAL EXPERIENCES

- Feeling comforted in their presence
  but slowly losing freedom.

- Realizing you let go of friendships or passions
  to keep the peace.

- Mistaking possession for protection.

- Learning the difference between love that nurtures
  and love that confines.

When have I attracted a Protector?

_____

_____

_____

_____

_____

_____

_____

_____

_____

_____

_____

What part of me was seeking something through them?

_____

_____

_____

_____

_____

_____

_____

_____

_____

_____

_____

_____

_____

_____

_____

_____

_____

_____

_____

_____

_____

What did this relationship mirror back to me?

_____

_____

_____

_____

_____

_____

_____

_____

_____

_____

_____

_____

_____

_____

_____

_____

_____

_____

_____

_____

_____

_____

_____

What did I gain in this connection?

_____

_____

_____

_____

_____

_____

_____

_____

_____

_____

_____

_____

_____

_____

_____

_____

_____

_____

_____

What did I lose in this connection?

_____

_____

_____

_____

_____

_____

_____

_____

_____

_____

_____

_____

_____

_____

_____

_____

_____

_____

_____

_____

MIRROR WORK

Stand in front of a mirror and say:

*"True love allows me to grow and expand
- not shrink or hide.."*

Take a moment to notice what emotions or resistance rise up. Write them here:

_____

_____

_____

_____

_____

_____

_____

_____

_____

_____

_____

_____

_____

_____

_____

_____

RELEASE RITUAL

Write a letter to the Protector archetype. Thank them for the lessons, acknowledge what you are releasing, and affirm your worthiness of love that feels aligned and whole.

_____

_____

_____

_____

_____

_____

_____

_____

_____

_____

_____

_____

_____

_____

_____

_____

_____

_____

"Every person you meet is a mirror,
showing you the parts of yourself waiting to be loved"

THE PARTY LOVER

The Party Lover is vibrant, fun, and magnetic in social spaces. Nights with them feel alive and exhilarating. Yet, when the music stops and the crowd fades, you may find their love doesn't stay.

POTENTIAL EXPERIENCES

- Experiencing wild nights of fun but lonely mornings after.
- Believing joy together in the moment meant longevity later.
- Being the responsible one while they sought constant escape.
- Learning that love cannot only live in fleeting highs.

When have I attracted a Party Lover?

_____

_____

_____

_____

_____

_____

_____

_____

_____

_____

_____

_____

_____

_____

What part of me was seeking something through them?

What did this relationship mirror back to me?

_____

_____

_____

_____

_____

_____

_____

_____

_____

_____

_____

_____

_____

_____

_____

_____

_____

_____

_____

_____

What did I gain in this connection?

_____

_____

_____

_____

_____

_____

_____

_____

_____

_____

_____

_____

_____

_____

_____

_____

_____

_____

_____

_____

_____

What did I lose in this connection?

MIRROR WORK

Stand in front of a mirror and say:

*"I am worthy of love
that stays after the music fades."*

Take a moment to notice what emotions or resistance rise up.
Write them here:

_____

_____

_____

_____

_____

_____

_____

_____

_____

_____

_____

_____

_____

_____

_____

_____

RELEASE RITUAL

Write a letter to the Party Lover archetype. Thank them for the
lessons, acknowledge what you are releasing, and affirm your
worthiness of love that feels aligned and whole.

_____

_____

_____

_____

_____

_____

_____

_____

_____

_____

_____

_____

_____

_____

_____

_____

_____

_____

*"Every person you meet is a mirror,
showing you the parts of yourself waiting to be loved"*

THE STORM

The Storm is intense, passionate, and unpredictable. One day they are radiant sunshine, the next day chaos and rage. Their love is intoxicating but unstable, leaving you walking on eggshells.

POTENTIAL EXPERIENCES

- Being swept up in passionate highs followed by painful lows.
- Confusing intensity with intimacy.
- Losing yourself in trying to manage their emotions.
- Realizing that peace feels safer than passion that burns too hot.

When have I attracted a Storm?

_____

_____

_____

_____

_____

_____

_____

_____

_____

_____

_____

_____

What part of me was seeking something through them?

_____

_____

_____

_____

_____

_____

_____

_____

_____

_____

_____

_____

_____

_____

_____

_____

_____

_____

_____

_____

_____

What did this relationship mirror back to me?

What did I gain in this connection?

_____

_____

_____

_____

_____

_____

_____

_____

_____

_____

_____

_____

_____

_____

_____

_____

_____

_____

_____

_____

What did I lose in this connection?

MIRROR WORK

Stand in front of a mirror and say:

> *"Love should not be a guessing game.*
> *I am worthy of calm, consistent love."*

Take a moment to notice what emotions or resistance rise up. Write them here:

_____

_____

_____

_____

_____

_____

_____

_____

_____

_____

_____

_____

_____

_____

RELEASE RITUAL

Write a letter to the Storm archetype. Thank them for the lessons, acknowledge what you are releasing, and affirm your worthiness of love that feels aligned and whole.

_____

_____

_____

_____

_____

_____

_____

_____

_____

_____

_____

_____

_____

_____

_____

_____

_____

_____

_____

_____

"Every person you meet is a mirror,
showing you the parts of yourself waiting to be loved"

THE NARCISSIST

The Narcissist is charming and magnetic at first, pulling you in with charisma and allure. But beneath the surface lies a heart closed to true intimacy. Their focus remains on themselves, leaving you unseen and unheard and fighting for attention.

POTENTIAL EXPERIENCES

- Being swept up in passionate highs followed by painful lows.

- Confusing intensity with intimacy.

- Losing yourself in trying to manage their emotions.

- Realizing that peace feels safer than passion that burns too hot.

When have I attracted a Narcissist?

_____

_____

_____

_____

_____

_____

_____

_____

_____

_____

What part of me was seeking something through them?

_____

_____

_____

_____

_____

_____

_____

_____

_____

_____

_____

_____

_____

_____

_____

_____

_____

_____

_____

_____

_____

What did this relationship mirror back to me?

What did I gain in this connection?

_____

_____

_____

_____

_____

_____

_____

_____

_____

_____

_____

_____

_____

_____

_____

_____

_____

_____

_____

_____

What did I lose in this connection?

_____

_____

_____

_____

_____

_____

_____

_____

_____

_____

_____

_____

_____

_____

_____

_____

_____

_____

_____

_____

_____

MIRROR WORK

Stand in front of a mirror and say:

*"I am worthy of mutual love
that flows both ways."*

Take a moment to notice what emotions or resistance rise up. Write them here:

_____

_____

_____

_____

_____

_____

_____

_____

_____

_____

_____

_____

_____

_____

_____

RELEASE RITUAL

Write a letter to the Narcissist archetype. Thank them for the lessons, acknowledge what you are releasing, and affirm your worthiness of love that feels aligned and whole.

_____

_____

_____

_____

_____

_____

_____

_____

_____

_____

_____

_____

_____

_____

_____

_____

_____

_____

_"Every person you meet is a mirror,
showing you the parts of yourself waiting to be loved"_

THE --

Not every love story fits a category, and not every teacher wears a name we already know. This page is for your unique archetype, a person, pattern, or energy that has shaped how you love, receive, protect, or express yourself.

Maybe this archetype showed up in a fleeting connection, or maybe they were part of a long, repeating cycle. Maybe they mirrored a part of you that still seeks attention, or revealed a lesson you didn't know you were ready to learn.

Whatever form they take, this archetype is your opportunity to bring another mirror into the light, one that belongs entirely to you.

DESCRIPTION

- Who is this archetype?

- What traits define them?

- How did their energy make you feel - seen, excited, unsafe, loved, challenged?

When have I attracted a -- ?

_____

_____

_____

_____

_____

_____

_____

_____

What part of me was seeking something through them?

_____

_____

_____

_____

_____

_____

_____

_____

_____

_____

_____

_____

_____

_____

_____

_____

_____

_____

_____

_____

_____

What did this relationship mirror back to me?

_____

_____

_____

_____

_____

_____

_____

_____

_____

_____

_____

_____

_____

_____

_____

_____

_____

_____

_____

_____

What did I gain in this connection?

What did I lose in this connection?

MIRROR WORK

Stand in front of a mirror and say:

"I forgive myself for the ways
I once accepted less than I deserved."

Take a moment to notice what emotions or resistance rise up.
Write them here:

_____

_____

_____

_____

_____

_____

_____

_____

_____

_____

_____

_____

_____

_____

_____

_____

RELEASE RITUAL

Write a letter to this archetype. Thank them for the wisdom they gave you and acknowledge the closure you're ready to claim. When you feel complete, you may tear, burn, or bury it as a symbol of release.

Affirmation:

"I am free from old patterns.
I carry forward only wisdom, love, and clarity."

_____

_____

_____

_____

_____

_____

_____

_____

_____

_____

_____

_____

_____

_____

_____

_____

_____

_____

_____

_____

_____

_____

_____

_____

_____

_____

_____

_____

_____

_____

_____

_____

_____

_____

_____

_____

_____

_____

"Every person you meet is a mirror,
showing you the parts of yourself waiting to be loved"

MIRROR WORK PRACTICES

The mirror has always been one of humanity's most powerful teachers. When you look into it, you are not only seeing your reflection, you are meeting your consciousness. Beneath the surface of your skin and the color of your eyes lives your story: every joy, every wound, every moment you turned away from yourself in search of love somewhere else.

Mirror work invites you to return to the source of your love - YOU. It is both gentle and radical: gentle because it asks only that you be present, and radical because it confronts the parts of you that you've been conditioned to hide. In this space, there is nowhere to run, nothing to fix, and no one to impress.

There is only truth - your truth.

The mirror shows what you believe about yourself. Sometimes it reflects tenderness and gratitude; other times, it reveals resistance, judgment, or sadness. All of it is sacred. When you can stand before your reflection and meet your own eyes with compassion, you begin to dissolve the illusions that have kept you separate from your worth.

These practices are not about vanity or perfection - they are about presence. They are about learning to witness yourself with love rather than criticism, to speak words of affirmation into the spaces where silence once lived, and to soften toward the parts of you that have been waiting to be seen.

As you move through this section, take your time. Let your breath guide you. Use the mirror as a sacred portal for communication between your outer self and your soul. Notice how your body feels, what emotions surface, and what thoughts arise. Allow yourself to stay open, even when it feels uncomfortable.

This is where transformation begins. Each exercise here is an opportunity to practice intimacy with yourself - the kind of intimacy that creates safety, confidence, and peace. As you deepen this relationship, you'll notice how your outer world begins to mirror the love you cultivate within.

So, find your mirror. Light a candle if you wish. Soften your gaze and open your heart. The person looking back at you is not your past, your pain, or your patterns. They are your becoming - the love you've been searching for all along.

MIRROR WORK EXERCISE 1

Sit with your reflection for several minutes. Breathe deeply and look softly into your own eyes. Allow whatever emotions arise to surface - tears, smiles, resistance, or peace.

Question: What do I see beyond my reflection?

Affirmation:

"I am safe in my own presence."

_____

_____

_____

_____

_____

_____

_____

_____

_____

_____

_____

_____

_____

_____

_____

_____

MIRROR WORK EXERCISE 2

Stand before the mirror and greet yourself as if you were meeting someone dear for the first time. Speak your name aloud and say:

"Hello, my love. It's good to see you again."

Notice how it feels to hear your own name spoken with kindness.

Question: How does it feel to meet myself with warmth?

Affirmation:

"I deserve my own gentleness."

_____

_____

_____

_____

_____

_____

_____

_____

_____

_____

_____

_____

_____

_____

_____

_____

_____

MIRROR WORK EXERCISE 3

"I see the parts of me I have hidden.
I see the parts of me I have judged."

Breathe deeply and imagine light filling those spaces.

Question: What part of me is asking to be seen today?

Affirmation:

"Every part of me is worthy of love."

_____

_____

_____

_____

_____

_____

_____

_____

_____

_____

_____

_____

_____

_____

_____

_____

MIRROR WORK EXERCISE 4

Hold your heart and imagine your younger self standing beside you in the mirror. Look into their eyes and say what they most needed to hear.

Question: What does my inner child need from me right now?

Affirmation:
> *"You are safe, loved, and never alone again."*

_____

_____

_____

_____

_____

_____

_____

_____

_____

_____

_____

_____

_____

_____

_____

_____

_____

_____

MIRROR WORK EXERCISE 5

"I forgive myself for not knowing what I didn't know."

Repeat until you feel a softening inside.

Question: What am I ready to forgive within myself?

Affirmation:

"Forgiveness frees me to love fully."

_____

_____

_____

_____

_____

_____

_____

_____

_____

_____

_____

_____

_____

_____

_____

_____

MIRROR WORK EXERCISE 6

Stand before the mirror and thank your body - each part that carries you, heals you, and holds your story.

"Thank you, arms, for holding. Thank you, legs, for walking. Thank you, heart, for feeling."

Question: Which part of my body deserves more gratitude today?

Affirmation:

"My body is a sacred home."

_____

_____

_____

_____

_____

_____

_____

_____

_____

_____

_____

_____

_____

_____

_____

_____

MIRROR WORK EXERCISE 7

Write 3-5 affirmations that speak directly to your healing journey. Stand in front of the mirror and say them slowly, making eye contact.

Examples:

- *"I am enough, exactly as I am."*

- *"I am becoming who I was always meant to be."*

- *"My love radiates from within."*

Question: Which affirmation feels the hardest to believe - and why?

Affirmation:
> *"I am learning to believe in my own light."*

_____

_____

_____

_____

_____

_____

_____

_____

_____

_____

_____

_____

MIRROR WORK EXERCISE 8

Gaze into the mirror and imagine you are looking at your future self, the one who has healed, grown, and stepped into love. Ask:

"What message do you have for me?"

Question: What did my future self say or show me?

Affirmation:

"I am already becoming who I am meant to be."

_____

_____

_____

_____

_____

_____

_____

_____

_____

_____

_____

_____

_____

_____

_____

_____

_____

_____

MIRROR WORK EXERCISE 9

Place your hand on your heart and look at yourself as you would someone you love deeply. Speak to yourself with compassion:

"You're doing your best. You've come so far."

Question: Which affirmation feels the hardest to believe - and why?

Affirmation:

"I am learning to believe in my own light."

_____

_____

_____

_____

_____

_____

_____

_____

_____

_____

_____

_____

_____

_____

_____

MIRROR WORK EXERCISE 10

Stand before the mirror and affirm your right to peace and energetic boundaries:

"I am allowed to take up space. I am allowed to say no?"

Visualize a soft golden light surrounding you as a loving boundary.

Question: What boundaries do I need to reinforce with love?

Affirmation:
"Protecting my energy is an act of self-respect."

_____

_____

_____

_____

_____

_____

_____

_____

_____

_____

_____

_____

_____

_____

MIRROR WORK EXERCISE II

Stand tall, shoulders back, and look into your own eyes. Speak your truth out loud:

> *"I am love. I am worthy. I am enough."*

Repeat until you feel it resonate in your body.

Question: What does unconditional self-love mean to me right now?

Affirmation:

> *"I am the love I have been searching for."*

_____

_____

_____

_____

_____

_____

_____

_____

_____

_____

_____

_____

_____

_____

SELF LOVE PRACTICES

You have looked into the mirrors of your relationships.
You have faced the shadows that shaped your patterns.
You have met your own eyes and begun to remember who you are.
Now it is time to embody that remembering, through love.
Self-love is not a destination or a single realization;
it is a daily practice of coming home to yourself.
It is the gentle act of choosing presence over perfection,
curiosity over criticism, and compassion over comparison.
It's theway you speak to yourself in quiet moments,
the care you give to your body,
and the boundaries you set to honor your peace.
For so long, love may have been something
you chased, proved, or earned.
These practices will help you experience love
as something you become. True love begins within,
not as an idea, but as an energy you live, breathe,
and extend to every part of your being.
Each exercise in this section invites you to cultivate
that love in real, tangible ways: through writing, reflection,
gratitude, visualization, and the daily rituals that restore
your sense of wholeness. There is no right or wrong way to move
through these pages. Follow your rhythm. Listen to your body.
Let your heart guide the pace.
Some practices will feel natural and joyful;
others might stretch you in new ways. All are designed to help
you anchor love as your foundation - not the conditional kind
that depends on someone else's presence or approval, but the
unconditional kind that flows from the truth of who you are.
As you journey through these pages, remember:
self-love is not selfish. It is sacred. The more you fill your own cup,
the more love overflows into your relationships,
your work, and your world.

So breathe. Soften. Receive.

Let these practices remind you that you were
never missing anything ... you were simply waiting
to return to yourself.

SELF LOVE PRACTICE 1

Write yourself a heartfelt love letter as if you were your own greatest partner. Tell yourself what you admire, forgive, and cherish. Read it aloud when you need to remember who you are.

Question: What do I most want to hear from someone who loves me deeply?

Affirmation:

"I am worthy of the words I long to receive."

_____

_____

_____

_____

_____

_____

_____

_____

_____

_____

_____

_____

_____

_____

_____

SELF LOVE PRACTICE 2

Draw yourself in the center of the page. Around you, list ten things you love or appreciate about who you are - qualities, quirks, gifts, even lessons learned through pain..

Question: What am I proud of in myself today?

Affirmation:

> *"Gratitude grows the garden of my heart."*

SELF LOVE PRACTICE 3

Close your eyes and imagine your future self - healed, peaceful, and radiant. What habits, boundaries, and joys define this version of you? Write their message to your current self.

Question: What wisdom does my future self want me to live now?

Affirmation:
   "I am already becoming who I am meant to be."

_____

_____

_____

_____

_____

_____

_____

_____

_____

_____

_____

_____

_____

_____

_____

_____

SELF LOVE PRACTICE 4

Begin each morning by looking into the mirror and choosing one word that captures how you want to feel today - calm, courageous, free. Speak it out loud three times.

Question: How does claiming this word shift my energy?

Affirmation:
  "Each morning, I choose my vibration."

_____

_____

_____

_____

_____

_____

_____

_____

_____

_____

_____

_____

_____

_____

_____

SELF LOVE PRACTICE 5

List five small, loving actions you can offer yourself this week - a nourishing meal, a walk in nature, a nap, saying "no," or asking for help. Then schedule them.

Question: Which act of self-devotion feels most revolutionary right now?

Affirmation:

"Caring for myself is holy work."

_____

_____

_____

_____

_____

_____

_____

_____

_____

_____

_____

_____

_____

_____

SELF LOVE PRACTICE 6

Think of an old belief that once limited your capacity for love (e.g., *"I'm too much," "I'm not enough"*).
Rewrite it in present tense as truth.

Question: What new story am I ready to live?

Affirmation:
"I am the author of my worth."

_____

_____

_____

_____

_____

_____

_____

_____

_____

_____

_____

_____

_____

_____

_____

_____

SELF LOVE PRACTICE 7

Place your hands on different parts of your body and speak gratitud:

*"Thank you, legs, for carrying me.
Thank you, heart, for feeling."*

Question: Which part of my body deserves more tenderness?

Affirmation:

"My body is my beloved home."

_____

_____

_____

_____

_____

_____

_____

_____

_____

_____

_____

_____

_____

_____

_____

SELF LOVE PRACTICE 8

Draw an energetic circle around your name on the page. Inside, write what nourishes you; outside, what drains you. Commit to honoring that boundary.

Question: What boundary keeps my peace intact?

Affirmation:

> *"Protecting my energy is an act of love."*

SELF LOVE PRACTICE 9

Make a list of moments that spark joy, big or small. Then plan to weave at least one into each day this week.

Question: What activities reconnect me to play and pleasure?

Affirmation:

"Joy is my birthright."

_____

_____

_____

_____

_____

_____

_____

_____

_____

_____

_____

_____

_____

_____

_____

_____

SELF LOVE PRACTICE 10

Stand with open palms and breathe in slowly, repeating:

"I am open to receive."

Question: Where do I resist receiving?

Affirmation:
"I allow love to find me and flow through me."

_____

_____

_____

_____

_____

_____

_____

_____

_____

_____

_____

_____

_____

_____

_____

SELF LOVE PRACTICE II

Light a candle and read this aloud in the mirror:

> *"I am the love I have been searching for.*
> *I honor my journey. I trust my becoming"*

Write your own closing declaration beneath it.

Question: What promise do I want to make to myself today?

Affirmation:
> *"My love for myself is unconditional and everlasting."*

_____

_____

_____

_____

_____

_____

_____

_____

_____

_____

_____

_____

_____

INTEGRATION & EMBODIMENT

You have journeyed through the mirrors of your relationships,
met your shadows with courage,
gazed deeply into your own eyes,
and opened to the truth of self-love.
Now, this final section is about integration.
Weaving together everything you've discovered
so that it becomes part of how you live,
breathe, and love every day.
Integration is where awareness becomes embodiment.
It is the sacred bridge between knowing and being.
You've done the deep inner work of remembering who you are;
now you allow that remembering to anchor
into your daily choices, your relationships,
your breath, and your presence.
**This is not the end of your healing,
it's the beginning of your wholeness.**
Integration is gentle and continual.
It asks for patience and compassion as you learn to walk
in the world as this new version of yourself.
Some days you'll feel radiant and grounded;
other days you'll revisit old stories
or slip into familiar patterns. That is natural.
Each time you return to your heart,
you are practicing integration.
In this space, you are invited to reflect on how your energy feels
now compared to when you began this journey.
Notice how you speak to yourself, how you respond to life,
and how you hold your boundaries.
Every shift, no matter how small,
is evidence of healing taking root.
These final pages are here for your reflections,
your intentions, your commitments to yourself.
Let them capture your truth in this moment.
A snapshot of the beautiful, evolving soul that you are.
Take your time. Breathe.
Let your transformation settle softly into your bones.

INTEGRATION EXERCISE I

At the start or end of each day, pause and ask yourself:

- What energy am I bringing into this moment?

- What does my body need right now?

- Am I acting from love or from fear?

Take three deep breaths and realign with your heart before you continue your day.

Question: How can I return to love in this moment?

Affirmation:
> *"Each breath brings me back to my center."*

_____

_____

_____

_____

_____

_____

_____

_____

_____

_____

_____

_____

INTEGRATION EXERCISE 2

Place your hand over your heart. Feel its rhythm - the quiet intelligence that has guided you through every chapter of your story. Speak aloud:

"I choose to live from this space."

Notice how your choices, tone, and relationships shift when you lead from love rather than protection.

Question: How can I listen to my heart more deeply today?

Affirmation:

"My heart is my compass."

_____

_____

_____

_____

_____

_____

_____

_____

_____

_____

_____

_____

_____

INTEGRATION EXERCISE 3

Stand in front of a mirror or close your eyes. Say the word "Yes" aloud and notice how your body responds expansion, warmth, openness.

Then say "No" and notice again - tension, constriction, grounding.

Your body always knows truth before your mind does.

Question: What does my "yes" feel like? What does my "no" feel like?

Affirmation:
>*"My body speaks my truth clearly and lovingly."*

_____

_____

_____

_____

_____

_____

_____

_____

_____

_____

_____

_____

_____

_____

INTEGRATION EXERCISE 4

Revisit each archetype you explored - The Adventurer, The Poet, The Protector, The Party Lover, The Storm, and The Narcissist.

For each one, ask:

- What did I learn from this energy?

- What gift did it offer me?

- How can I integrate its wisdom without its pain?

Write one sentence of gratitude to each archetype for its lesson.

Question: What part of each archetype now lives in balance within me?

Affirmation:
> *"I honor every teacher that shaped me."*

_____

_____

_____

_____

_____

_____

_____

_____

_____

_____

INTEGRATION EXERCISE 5

Transformation becomes lasting when it is woven into your daily life. Create one ritual that reminds you of your wholeness:

- Lighting a candle each morning
- Journaling before bed
- Placing your hand on your heart before speaking
- Practicing weekly mirror work

Question: What daily ritual will help me embody my love and truth?

Affirmation:

"My life itself is a sacred ceremony."

_____

_____

_____

_____

_____

_____

_____

_____

_____

_____

_____

INTEGRATION EXERCISE 6

Close your eyes and imagine your life as a vibrant tapestry, every relationship, experience, and lesson is a thread. Some are bright, some dark, all essential.

Now, visualize yourself standing in the center of that tapestry, radiant, whole, and at peace.

What does this version of you believe, say, and do?

Question: How does wholeness feel in my body and in my choices?

Affirmation:
   "I am the living embodiment of love and awareness."

_____

_____

_____

_____

_____

_____

_____

_____

_____

_____

_____

_____

_____

THE JOURNEY HOME TO YOU

Take a moment to close your eyes.
Feel your heartbeat. Feel your breath.
You have walked through the stories that shaped you,
through the loves that taught you,
and through the mirrors that revealed you.
You have looked into your own reflection and chosen to stay.
That choice to remain with yourself,
is the greatest act of love there is.
This work is not about perfection;
it is about presence.
It's about remembering that you are both the student
and the teacher, the question and the answer,
the lover and the beloved.
Everything you were seeking in another
was always waiting within you.
As you step beyond these pages,
may you carry this truth in your heart:
You are whole. You are worthy. You are love.
Not because you earned it,
but because it is what you have always been.
Continue to speak to yourself with kindness.
Continue to honor your needs.
Continue to pause before the mirror and whisper,
"I am here. I choose me."
Let your healing ripple outward, through your relationships,
your work, your laughter, your quiet moments.
The more you love yourself,
the more love you bring into the world.
When you forget, return.
When you fall, soften.
When you shine, expand.
This is your sacred rhythm of becoming.

A Note of Gratitude

From the depths of my heart ....
thank you.
Thank you for trusting me
to walk beside you in this sacred work.
Thank you for opening your heart,
for facing your reflection with honesty,
and for allowing yourself to be seen
and loved, by you.
Every page you've written,
every truth you've faced,
and every tear or smile
that found its way to these pages
has created ripples of healing in the collective.
Your courage to do this work
not only transforms you,
it transforms the world.
It has been my deepest honor
to guide you back home to yourself.
May you continue to walk this path
with grace, tenderness,
and unshakable faith in your own light.

With infinite love and gratitude,
Dr. Shine ♡
www.drshinekc.com

www.ingramcontent.com/pod-product-compliance
Lightning Source LLC
Chambersburg PA
CBHW070626130626
46555CB00006B/2463